LUNDY'S ARC

A History and Field Guide

by

Chris Webster

First published 2023

www.lundy.org.uk

© Chris Webster and the Lundy Field Society

Unless otherwise stated, reproduction of excerpts from this publication for educational or other non-commercial purposes is authorised without prior written permission from the copyright holder provided the source is fully acknowledged. Reproduction of this publication or any part of it for resale or other commercial purposes is prohibited without prior written permission of the copyright holder.

ISBN 978-0-9530532-8-5

Timeline of the periods covered in this book

Period	Lundy	Elsewhere in south-west Britain
Palaeolithic 700,000–8000 BCE	No evidence	Hunter-gatherers following seasonal food sources during inter-glacial periods
Mesolithic 8000–4000 BCE	Flint scatters and debitage	Hunter-gatherers following seasonal food sources
Neolithic 4000–2000 BCE	Some flints	Permanent farming settlements. Pottery. Megalithic sites such as Stonehenge, Avebury, etc.
Bronze Age 2000–800 BCE	Hut circles, standing stones, field systems, pottery	Landscape divided up into fields with permanent settlements. Origins of hillforts. Metalworking
Iron Age 800 BCE–43 CE	Some pottery	Iron tools as well as bronze. Hillforts develop, as well as smaller defended enclosures
Roman 43–410 CE	Scarce pottery	Britain part of the Roman empire with varying degrees of Romanisation. Money economy, new religions including Christianity introduced
Early Medieval 410–1066 CE	Beacon Hill memorial stones (5th/6th centuries)	Roman empire collapses, leading to smaller political units, some controlled by English immigrants. Christianity spreads. Later, Viking attacks lead to the formation of England and Wales
Medieval 1066–1540 CE	Castle. Farming settlements such as Widows Tenement established	Norman conquest. Towns and cities develop. Castles, cathedrals and other major buildings
Post-medieval 1540–1760 CE	Defences such as Brazen Ward	Growth of towns, agricultural improvements, international wars. English Civil War
Industrial/ Modern 1760 CE–now	Old House. The Quarries and jetty, Old Light and Fog Battery. Wreck of HMS Montagu. Admiralty lookout. Anti-aircraft trenches, crashed aircraft	New power sources, increased wealth for some, international trade and empire. First and Second World Wars

INTRODUCTION

ISLANDS hold a particular fascination for people, and more so for archaeologists as they appear self-contained with obvious limits to the area that can be studied. They also tend to be attractive and adventurous places to explore. Lundy is no exception, and this is the third archaeological guide to the island, covering over a century of work. The first was by Keith Gardner in 1972, written after the end of his decade-long series of expeditions to survey and excavate. This was followed by a shorter booklet by Caroline Thackray and Shirley Blaylock, published in 2002, showcasing the results of the National Trust's archaeological survey over the previous 10 years. Both are now out of print and this book is intended to provide a modern view of the archaeology and archaeologists of Lundy for visitors to the island.

Note that some of the sites in this book are close to steep cliffs and great care should be taken when approaching them. Some, such as Montagu Steps, should not be approached as they are unsafe. Additionally, consideration should be given at all times to the island's wildlife. The warden can provide advice on areas to avoid at certain times of year.

Most of the archaeological sites are protected, not just by their ownership by the National Trust and management by the Landmark Trust, but legally as Scheduled Monuments, Protected Wrecks or Listed Buildings. Please do not disturb them by climbing on ruined walls or moving loose stones.

Bronze Age barbed and tanged flint arrowhead found by chance at the North End in 1970. 33mm x 22mm. Privately owned

Cover illustrations
Top: the Castle. Bottom: plan of the Castle from Grose's 'Antiquities of England and Wales'. Inserts, top to bottom: Beacon Hill memorial stones, Fog Battery, a millstone

People on Lundy

THE earliest signs of people on Lundy date from about 8000 BCE, when the climate of northern Europe was warming after the Ice Age. Large amounts of water were still frozen as ice sheets so the sea level would have been very much lower than today, and Lundy would have been much larger, though still with the present island rising as a large hill above the lower ground. It is not certain if the sea level was low enough for Lundy to have joined the mainland, but it is possible. These Mesolithic (middle stone age) people would have led a nomadic lifestyle moving with the seasons as the animals they hunted migrated. The only signs we have of their presence are scatters of stone tools, and the waste from making them (known as debitage), which survive in the modern soil on the island. We have no idea what they did in the areas that are now below the sea, but the present Lundy would have provided extensive views across the lowlands that might have been useful for seeking out migrating herds of wild cattle and deer. Settlements of this date are extremely rare survivals and none is known from Lundy.

There is similarly limited evidence for the succeeding Neolithic (new stone age, from about 4000 BCE) period with small numbers of characteristic stone tools again the only evidence. On the mainland great changes are seen, with cereal cultivation, pottery and the construction of large monuments for the first time. It has been suggested that there was a chambered tomb (the Kistvaen) from this period at the south end of the island but the evidence for this is inconclusive.

The first metalwork appears in about 2400 BCE signifying a complex series of changes that continue through the early Bronze Age. Very little material of this date has been found on Lundy but some of the mounds and cairns on the island may be funerary monuments from this time.

A significant change is seen in the Middle Bronze Age with the beginnings of a more settled lifestyle when permanent settlements were constructed and fields laid out around them. Pottery of this date has been found in a round house at the North End but most of the other houses appear to date from the Late Bronze Age.

Most of the prehistoric pottery found on Lundy has been of Late Bronze Age date, from stone-built round houses and enclosures at the North End, Widows Tenement, Middle Park and Beacon Hill. This last site has produced evidence for the specialised pottery vessels used for salt production, known as briquetage.

There is no evidence from Lundy from the Iron Age, apart from a single sherd of pottery from the North End which appears to be in the South West Decorated Ware tradition, dated to the last three centuries BCE in Devon. All the prehistoric pottery appears to have been made on the island, so small sherds without distinctive features could be of any date.

A small amount of Roman pottery was excavated from below the cemetery on Beacon Hill which appeared to be related to a circular structure that probably began as a Late Bronze Age round house. This suggests the possibility of a small farm on the island. Very little other Roman material has been found away from this area suggesting that it may have been the only settlement on the island at this time.

The Beacon Hill settlement may have continued into the following fifth and sixth centuries when it seems to have become a Christian monastery with links to South Wales and North Devon. Excavations in the cemetery have revealed stone-lined graves similar to other examples of this date but this Early Medieval period is very hard to study in western Britain as people seem to have used few distinctive artefacts or structures.

In the thirteenth century Lundy emerges into history with the building of a castle by King Henry III in the 1240s, following the rebellion of William de Marisco. Earlier that century, a title grant mentions two settlements, one probably Widows Tenement, and also common pasture on the island that must have been shared with at least one other settlement, probably under the current village.

The relatively large population implied by these settlements, and the castle garrison recorded later, did not remain as by the late fifteenth century the island is reported to be uninhabited and may have been so for a century. Subsequently the island became noted as a base for pirates, who are recorded as raiding the neighbouring coasts, but a description of the island in the earlier seventeenth century suggests that it was again enjoying more settled times under Sir Bevill Grenville who built a pier amongst other improvements.

In the Civil War (1640s) the island was held for the king by Thomas Bushell, who claimed afterwards to have built the castle; certainly, all that is visible today looks to be of this date. Another period of piracy followed until the mid-eighteenth century when Thomas Benson used the island to house convicts that he should have transported to America. The convicts laboured to build a wall across the island and were housed in the castle. Benson's activities came to an end when he was caught undertaking an insurance fraud and fled to Portugal. Lundy seems to have fallen on hard times again until bought in 1775 by Sir John Borlase Warren who repaired Grenville's house and built another that survives as Old House in the village. Warren had further investment plans, including a mansion house, but substantial debts forced him to sell the island.

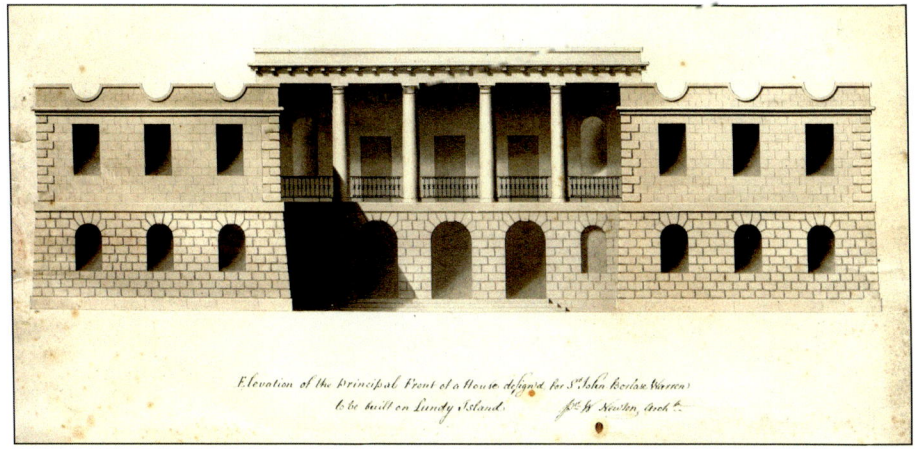

The front of the house that Sir John Borlase Warren had designed for Lundy by the London architect William Newton

Further significant changes took place at the beginning of the nineteenth century when Trinity House built a lighthouse on the high ground at Beacon Hill, with accommodation for the keepers and visiting officials (now Old Light and Stoneycroft). In 1836 the island was bought by William Hudson Heaven, using his government compensation for freed Jamaican slaves, and improvements were implemented to make it suitable for periodic visits by the owner. He built a villa (now Millcombe House) in a sheltered position, renovated the farmhouse and built houses for farm labourers inside the keep of the castle. Trinity House improved the lighthouse, which was often obscured by clouds, and then built a fog station to produce audible warnings. In the 1860s, Heaven leased most of the island for granite quarrying which has left significant remains on the east side and numerous other buildings. The granite company also redesigned the layout of the fields between the village and Quarter Wall.

In the 1890s, a stone church was built to replace a prefabricated corrugated iron one that had been built in 1885, and Trinity House accepted that the position of the lighthouse was unsuitable, replacing it with two low-level lights at the north and south ends of the island.

The twentieth century saw an increase in the use of the island for tourism, culminating in the purchase of Lundy by the National Trust, funded by Sir Jack Hayward, and its leasing to the Landmark Trust. New buildings and some demolitions have changed the village area and that around the castle.

Marker stone erected by Trinity House at the bottom of the Beach Road in 1819 when they arrived to build what is now the Old Light

Archaeologists on Lundy

THE earliest antiquarian interest in Lundy was shown by Francis Grose in the 1770s. He didn't visit the island but had a report from a gentleman who lists the 'ancient buildings' as the castle, St Helen's chapel 'ruined to the foundations', the remains of a house near St Helen's Well and two watch towers. St Helen's chapel is presumably the small building in Beacon Hill cemetery. Grose notes two walls across the island and also many ruined walls that showed that Lundy had once been cultivated. The castle is described as having large outworks and surrounded by a ditch. Grose provides two engraved views and a plan of the castle.

In the nineteenth century, two discoveries were reported, the Giants Graves and the Kistvaen, but these don't seem to have attracted much knowledgeable interest at the time. In 1928, the naturalist WS Bristowe followed up the Giants Graves story and discovered further burials as did, in 1933, the young geologist ATJ Dollar and the eccentric archaeologist TC Lethbridge, who had met on an expedition to the Arctic.

Keith Gardner first visited Lundy in 1955 and spent the next few years locating and surveying sites before excavating a mound in 1961, close to the earlier finds of burials. No further burials were found so Gardner moved to an earthwork further south in Bulls Paradise where he excavated walls that he interpreted as the stronghold of the Mariscos. He and Trevor Miles returned to this site for several years but also carried out small excavations on other sites, primarily to obtain dating evidence. When Lundy was put up for sale in 1969, Gardner, fearing that he would not be allowed to continue, organised a final season, persuading Charles Thomas to excavate in the Beacon Hill cemetery and Peter Fowler to examine a linear bank just south of it. None of this work produced a formal publication but several interim statements were issued.

Keith Gardner leading a tour in 1996

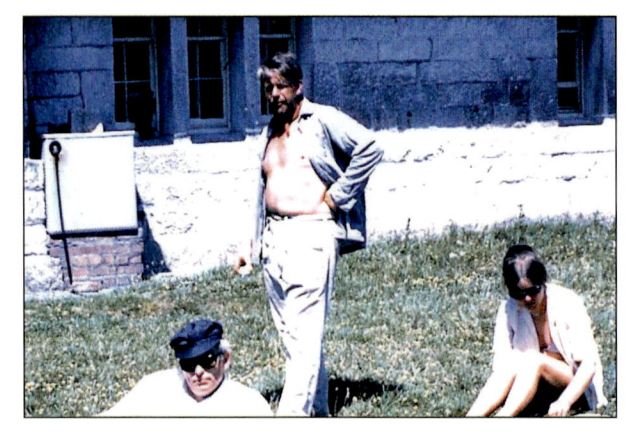

Charles Thomas and some of his team outside the Old Light

Following the purchase of the island, further work was carried out by the National Trust's archaeological staff, principally David and Caroline Thackray. This led to excavations at the castle in 1978 and 1984-85 and to a large-scale survey of the remains on the island from 1990 to 1994. Most of this work remains unpublished.

Some independent work took place between 1989 and 1990, when John Schofield and Chris Webster used test-pits and geophysical surveys to discover sites in the pasture south of Quarter Wall. Recording of a service trench across Pigs Paradise by Shirley Blaylock in 2000 led to reports on the pottery from here and other sites by John Allen in 2005 and to research into Gardner's prehistoric finds by Henrietta Quinnell in 2010. Most recently, Chris Webster has started to write up Gardner's excavations based on the records left by Gardner and Miles, the first report on which was published in the Lundy Field Society *Journal* in 2020.

Left to right: Shirley Blaylock, Chris Webster and Henrietta Quinnell leading an archaeological walk on Lundy during the Lundy Field Society's 'Discover Lundy' Week in May 2012

Sites to Visit

These are listed roughly from south to north. The numbers in square brackets are the site numbers in the National Trust's record which can be accessed at *https://heritagerecords.nationaltrust.org.uk/home* for further information – or scan the QR code.

Castle [108759] *(plan on next page)*

Most, if not all, that can be seen dates to the Civil War of the seventeenth century following which the governor, Thomas Bushell, claimed to have built it from the ground up. It comprises a level platform with angle bastions, the excavated ruins of a house, some brick buildings next to the house and the so-called keep now converted to cottages. The origins of the castle lie, however, in the thirteenth century when King Henry III ordered a 'tower with a bailey wall' to be built in 1243 following the capture of William de Marisco. To the north, a ditch is visible, curving up from the cliff face, which may be the outer defences of the medieval castle. It is possible that this ditch originated earlier, perhaps in the Iron Age, as there is no mention of a large workforce being recruited to dig it in the medieval records. It is not clear if the keep, a curious structure with few parallels, is the medieval tower, and excavations in the 1980s failed to resolve this. The house is believed to have been built by Bushell as part of his works at the castle and was also excavated in the 1980s. The brick buildings around it seem to have had an industrial function with a furnace and a complex series of drains.

The complex walls and floor surfaces exposed by excavation outside Castle House in 1985

To the west, two cottages were built in the late nineteenth century for signallers employed by Lloyds of London who reported by undersea cable on the passing shipping. A signalling flagpole was erected near the Old House and a flag storage hut was built adjacent. A row of coastguard cottages was built on the north side of the track in 1906. All these have been demolished except for the cable hut, built on the side of the castle, which was extended to form a holiday cottage.

The site of Castle House before excavation with the Lloyds signal store behind

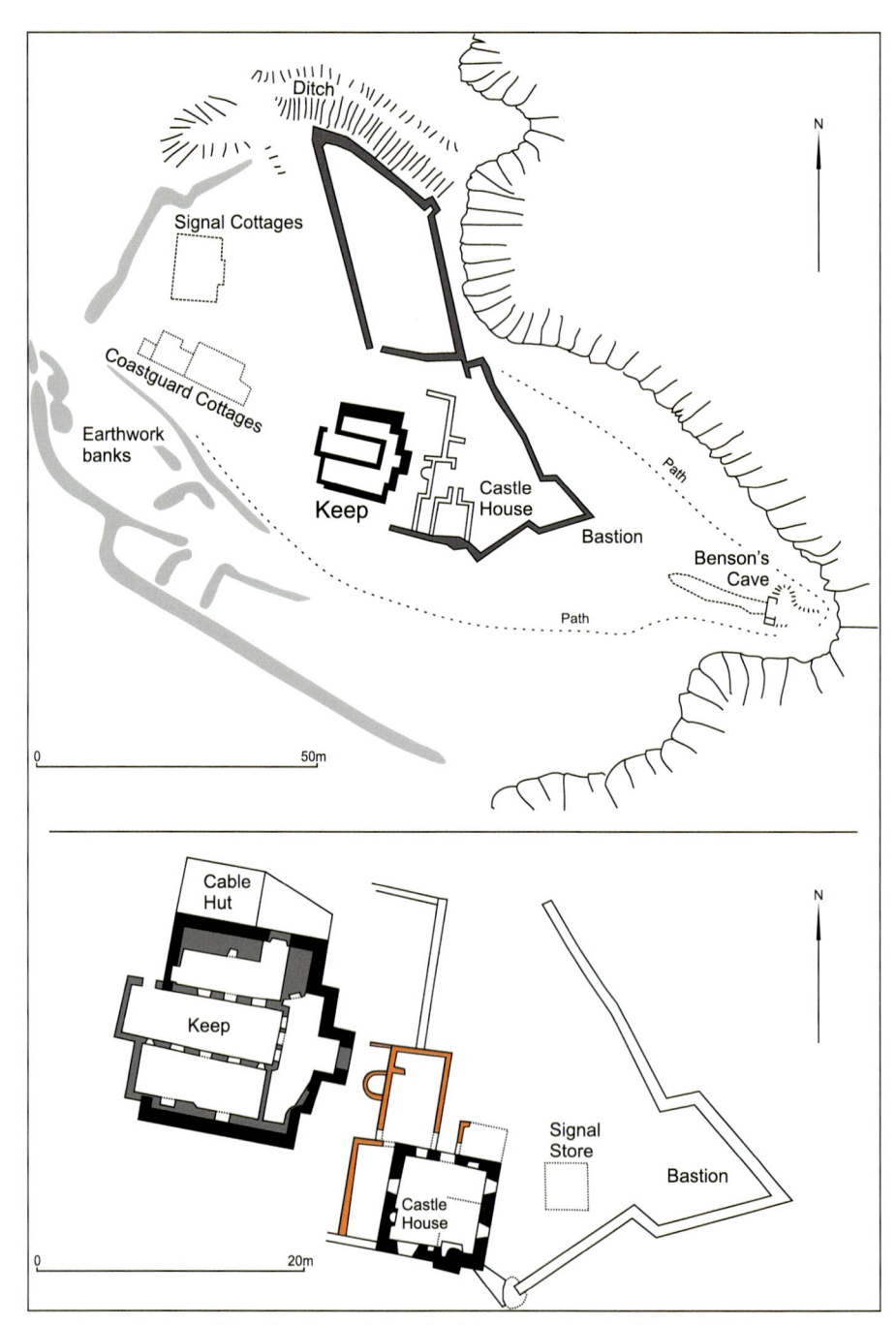

Overall plan of the Castle and detail of the surviving buildings (19th-century additions to the keep in grey; post-medieval brick-built buildings in orange)

- page 10 -

Benson's Cave [108759]

On the very edge of the cliff, to the east and below the castle, is a large artificial cave. The entrance is low with the remains of a brick building on the south side and suggestions in the masonry that another building stood above the entrance. Inside, the cave is wide with a very high roof for no apparent reason. The most obvious creator of the cave is Thomas Bushell, who was a mining engineer, but its purpose is unclear. It would have made a well-concealed store but access to and from it would have been inconvenient. The name refers to a later owner of Lundy, who housed convicts in the castle, and the initials of some have been found carved in the cave.

Recording the excavations in the entrance to Benson's Cave in 1966

Graffiti in Benson's Cave

Chambered tomb – the Kistvaen [108749, 108750]

The Kistvaen, or is it?

The 1886 Ordnance Survey map shows a rectangular area as 'Kistvaen (Remains of)' containing some small ponds and having the appearance of a granite trial pit. This site was discovered in 1851 when a large slab of granite was found covering a cavity 1.8m deep and wide. Nothing was found to suggest a date and the capstone was subsequently split and used as gateposts. The naturalist Philip Gosse saw it in 1852 and compared it to Wayland's Smithy, a well-known Neolithic chambered tomb in Berkshire. Later editions of the map show the name further to the east where a mound is shown and where currently a rectangular pit is visible in the vegetation. Gosse's description indicates that the chamber lay below ground, whereas chambered cairns usually have chambers that were built at ground level and then covered by a mound. The situation is further complicated by the description kistvaen (from the Welsh 'stone chest') which would apply better to the rectangular pit; similar Bronze Age examples are known from Dartmoor.

Rocket Pole [108752]

Once a common sight around the coast, this post was used to practise life-saving drills, based on the use of rockets to take a rope out to a stranded vessel. The equipment was stored in the Rocket Shed in the village, now the museum. The adjacent pond was dug for stone to build the South Light.

Rocket Pole Pond with the pole at the rear

HMS Montagu [108335]

In 1906 HMS Montagu struck Lundy in thick fog while testing new radio equipment. No lives were lost and much of the equipment of the ship was salvaged before she sank. The hull survives below the water and the base of an aerial ropeway used to bring salvage onto the island can be seen a short way down a steep path.

There are also some concrete steps that were built in about 1918 when a new owner, Augustus Christie, wanted to make a landing place on the west side. The steps are known as the Montagu Steps after the earlier wreck but are now dangerous as the handrails have been lost to corrosion.

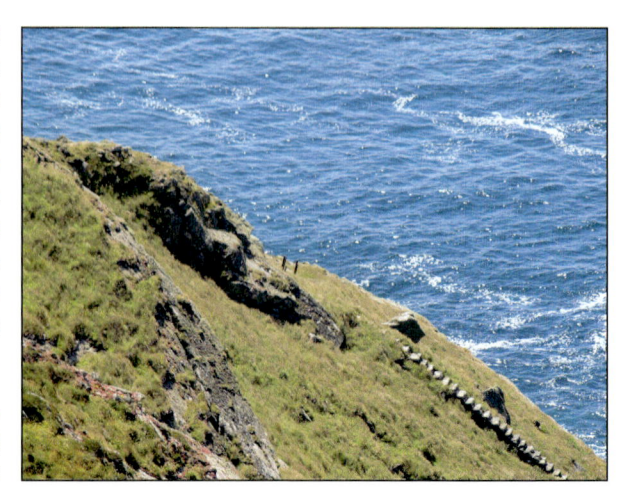

HMS Montagu fast on the rocks and undergoing salvage

The Montagu Steps built by AL Christie in about 1918 to allow west side landings

- page 12 -

Village

The village seems to have been the focus of settlement on Lundy since the medieval period but the oldest standing building is Old House, probably built for Sir John Borlase Warren in the 1770s. Most of the other buildings were built by the Lundy Granite Company in the 1860s or by the tenant farmer in the 1880s. Old House was extended by the granite company and this part was made into a hotel in the early years of the twentieth century. The hotel expanded to include Old House in the 1920s but was partly demolished by the Landmark Trust in the 1970s and replaced by Square Cottage. Other buildings in the village have been converted to accommodation, the shop and a small museum.

Excavations in the camping field (Pigs Paradise) and the field to the north (Bulls Paradise) since the 1960s have recorded walls and recovered large amounts of medieval and post-medieval pottery. These walls have been interpreted as the stronghold of William de Marisco but the small area excavated makes this interpretation uncertain.

The excavation in Bulls Paradise, probably in 1969. Deep ditches and substantial walls are visible but the overall plan is unclear

Giants Graves [108651]

In 1856 workmen digging foundation trenches for a new farm building uncovered several skeletons, one of which was said to be over eight feet tall (2.4m). There is only one contemporary account which says the bones crumbled before they could be measured, so the extreme height must have been assumed from the length of the skeleton in the ground, which usually over-emphasises stature. The 'giant' is reported to have been buried in a stone chamber or cist with a hollowed stone forming a pillow. A stone purporting to be the pillow is now in the church porch, but again the early descriptions do not entirely support this identification. Subsequent publications embellished the story so that the truth is hard to determine but twentieth-century excavations uncovered other burials under stone slabs that were dated to the post-medieval period.

Anti-aircraft trenches [eg 108549]

During the Second World War there was a fear of invasion or raids from the air, and fields all over the country were obstructed with posts, felled trees, earth mounds and ditches. They are usually called anti-glider trenches but were actually to prevent powered aircraft taking off again to collect more supplies. Most were removed during the war, as agricultural production became a higher priority than fear of invasion, but some survive on Lundy.

The partly infilled remains of an anti-aircraft obstruction, south of Beacon Hill

New Town [108743]

Early nineteenth-century maps show an area on the cliff edge north of the village as New Town and test-pit excavations in the 1980s recorded a concentration of post-medieval pottery here. This may be the settlement established by Sir John Borlase Warren in the 1770s when he intended to encourage Shetlanders to settle on the island, but the picture is confused by another area known as New Town at the north end of the village.

Old Light [109310]

Lundy has always been a danger to shipping and a group of Bristol merchants proposed building a lighthouse on Beacon Hill in the late eighteenth century. This came to nothing until 1819 when Trinity House acquired the site and built a 30m tall lighthouse with attached accommodation for the keepers. The architect was Daniel Alexander who built a number of lighthouses and also designed Dartmoor Prison. The light, the highest in Britain, was often obscured by low cloud and it was augmented by the fog battery in 1863. They were replaced by the North and South Lights in the 1890s.

The Old Light

Cemetery on Beacon Hill [108931]

Four inscribed stones are known from the cemetery, one found in 1905 when digging a grave and the other three following a concerted search in the early 1960s. These are of a type well-known in Wales and Cornwall and are believed to be early Christian gravestones.

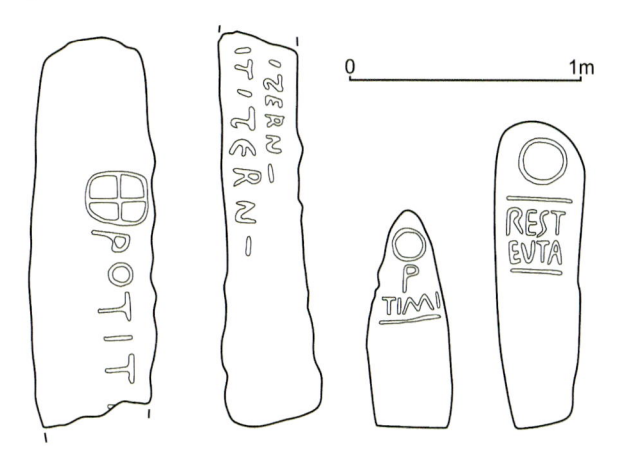

The early Christian stones from Beacon Hill

Two of the stones have male Roman names, Potitus and Optimus, while Resteuta appears to have been female and had a British name. These are believed to date from the fifth century, while the damaged fourth stone reading [...]IGERN [FIL]I TIGERNI, ([...] igern son of Tigernus) is probably from the sixth century. The single-name stones are believed to have been memorials to people who gave up their earthly families to take up a religious life. Excavations in 1969 recorded numerous slab-lined graves, of early medieval character, clustering around a burial that appeared to have been removed. Charles Thomas suggested that this burial was of the founder of the monastery, whose relics were later taken to the mainland, possibly to the monastery at Hartland.

To the north are the ruined walls of a small chapel. This has been excavated several times but no dating evidence was recovered.

Four of the cist graves in Beacon Hill cemetery with the wall surrounding an important burial behind them

MAP OF LUNDY

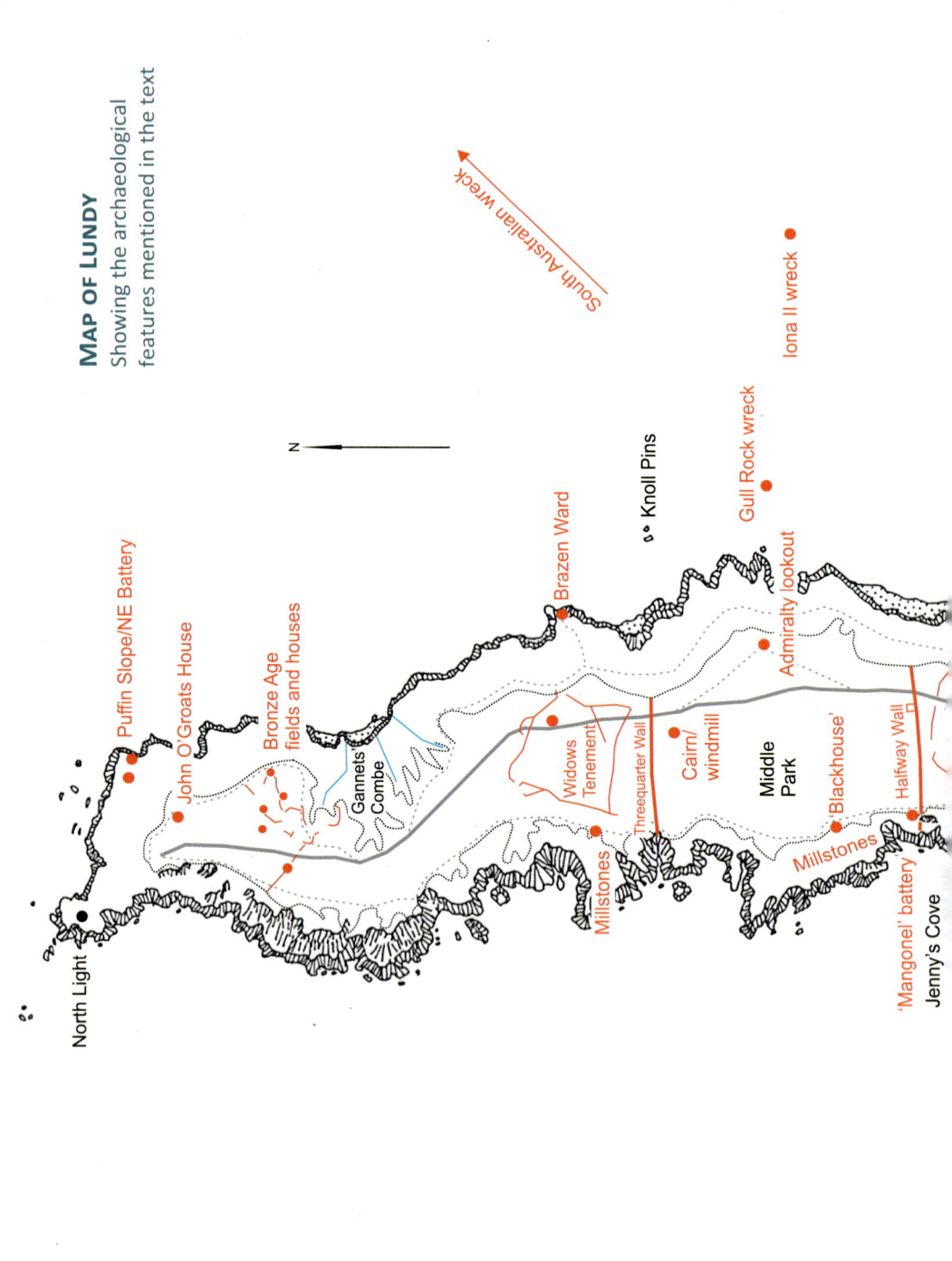

Showing the archaeological features mentioned in the text

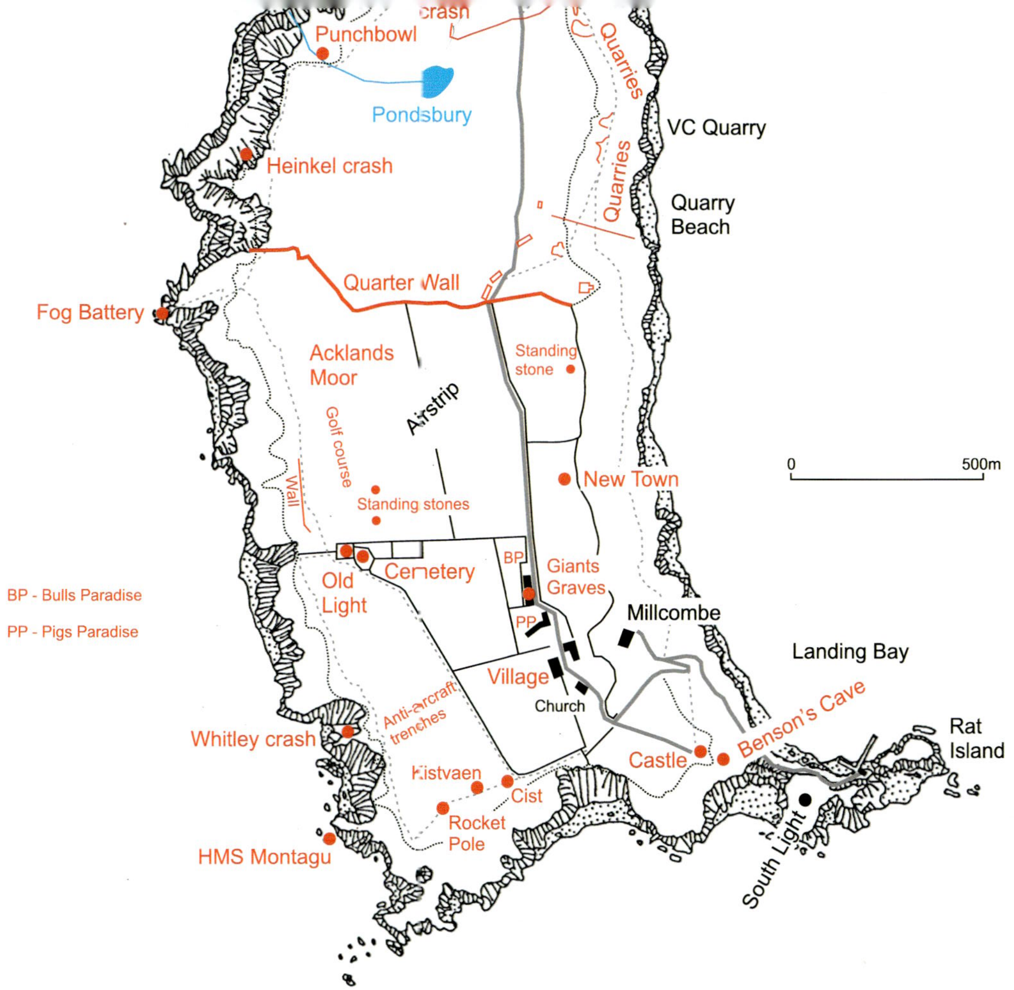
crash
Punchbowl
Pondsbury
Heinkel crash
Quarries
Quarries
VC Quarry
Quarry Beach
Quarter Wall
Fog Battery
Acklands Moor
Airstrip
Standing stone
Golf course
Wall
Standing stones
New Town
0
500m
Old Light
Cemetery
BP
Giants Graves
PP
Millcombe
Landing Bay
Village
Church
Anti-aircraft trenches
Whitley crash
Kistvaen
Cist
Rocket Pole
Castle
Benson's Cave
Rat Island
South Light
HMS Montagu
BP - Bulls Paradise
PP - Pigs Paradise

Acklands Moor [various]

There are several standing stones on Lundy, including one [108463] just to the north-east of the Old Light, another [108467] 100m to the north and a third on the east side in Brick Field [108642]. These are believed to date from the Bronze Age and various suggestions have been put forward to explain them, including burial markers and sighting marks for celestial events. Few burials have been found associated with ones that have been excavated, and there is a large number of celestial events that could be indicated, even without taking into account the probably large number of stones that have been removed in the thousands of years since their erection.

The standing stones to the north of the Old Light (left) and in Brick Field (right)

Other smaller stones are visible that have been suggested as parts of stone circles but are more likely to be the remains of kerbs surrounding burial cairns. A double row of stones along the cliff top on the west side is the remains of a relatively recent wall [108401] as shown by the presence of quarrying jumper holes on at least one stone. It appears unfinished and may have been built by Trinity House to protect the route to the fog battery or by WH Heaven to try to exclude rabbits.

To add to the confusion on Acklands Moor, a golf course [108362] was constructed here in 1926/27 with hopes of attracting visiting golfers. The membership never exceeded twelve and the course was abandoned after the 1928 season. Occasional games have been played since and the earthworks of some tees are still visible.

Fog Battery [108429]

The battery was constructed in 1863 to provide audible warning to ships when the Old Light was obscured by low cloud. There were two cottages for the Trinity House staff and their families, each with an outside toilet. Originally, two obsolete cannon were fired to produce the warning noise but these were later replaced by rockets.

The Fog Battery

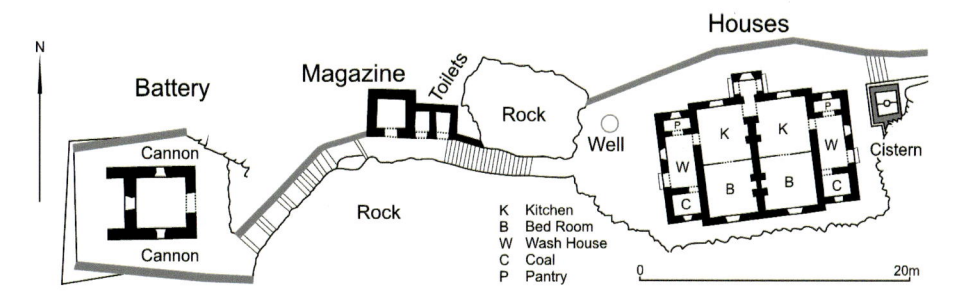

Plan of the fog battery and accommodation

Quarter Wall [108361]
Quarter Wall is the oldest of the walls across the island and old maps show that its irregular course was dictated by the shape of the small fields to the south. These fields have been abandoned on the west side but some of the ruined walls are visible as earthworks. To the east, the granite company replaced the small fields by larger fields with the straight boundaries that survive today. Quarter Wall itself is an earth bank retained by stone walling to either side. In Cornwall, some walls like this have survived from the Bronze Age, and Quarter Wall could be similarly ancient.

Quarter Wall has possibly been here since the Bronze Age

Quarries [various] *(plan on next page)*
Most of the island was leased to the newly established Lundy Granite Company in 1863, who built a small settlement just to the north of Quarter Wall as well as improving the farm and buildings in the village. Three rows of cottages for workers were built close to the track but only two were ever completed and they have all been demolished leaving only low walls. A datestone of 1864 was found during work near Quarter Wall that presumably came from these cottages. Three houses were constructed further east for the quarry officials and these survive as roofless ruins. To the north they built a hospital and surgery, parts of which survive.

Some 200 men were employed at the quarry's height. The granite was quarried from several large quarries, linked by a tramway and lowered to a new quay down an inclined plane. The large platform constructed for stone dressing is accessible with the inclined planes visible at the south end. The foundations of the quay can be seen on the beach, though access is not always possible. In 1868, the company suddenly went into liquidation, leading to a period of legal wrangling and the dilapidation of many of the buildings.

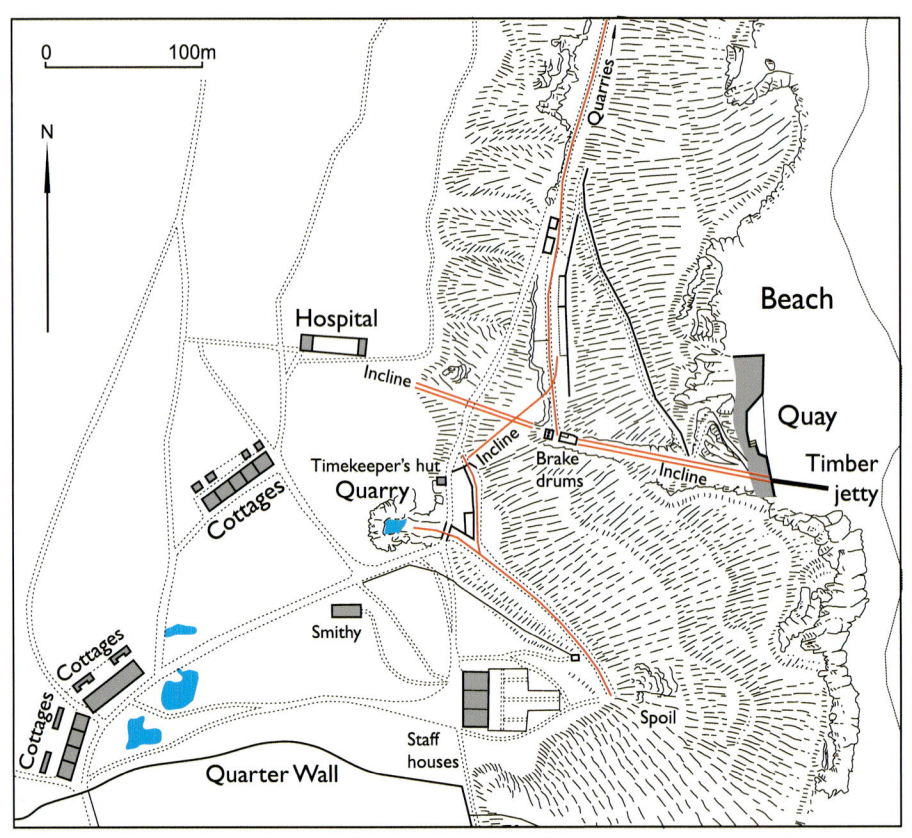

Plan of the southern end of the complex of quarries operated by the Lundy Granite Company. Red lines are tramways

The surviving building of the Quarry Company's medical facilities

View along the Quarry terrace from the south

VC Quarry has been known by this name since 1949 as it contains a memorial to the owner's son, John Pennington Harman VC, who died at Kohima in 1944

Medieval farm [108264]
An area of small fields and some buildings, surviving as low grass-covered banks, has been suggested to be a medieval farm. There is certainly evidence of characteristic ridge-and-furrow cultivation but excavation in 1966 produced only prehistoric pottery.

Punchbowl [108315]
By the side of the stream that higher up has been dammed to form Pondsbury is a circular granite bowl. It was first mentioned in 1775 but no satisfactory interpretation was offered then, or has been since. It has been broken and repaired several times.

The Punchbowl

Aircraft crash sites [various]

Three aircraft crashed on Lundy during the Second World War, two German Heinkel 111s within a month in 1941 and one British Whitley in 1942. The first Heinkel [108260] touched down less than 100m north of Quarter Wall and came to a halt 200m south of Halfway Wall. The crew all survived and set fire to the plane. The second Heinkel crashed into the top of the cliffs on the west side and burst into flames, leaving two dead and one injured of the five man crew. The Whitley [109413] was returning to RAF Chivenor from an anti-submarine patrol and flew into the island in poor visibility; there were no survivors. There are a few remains of the first Heinkel but much has been removed by souvenir hunters. A crankshaft of the second Heinkel remains lodged in rocks.

Left: the first Heinkel, south of Halfway Wall. Right: the second Heinkel on the west side

Halfway Wall [108228]

The wall was started by Thomas Benson in 1752, using convict labour, but it is believed that it was finished as part of Sir John Borlase Warren's improvements later in the century. It was known as North Wall before Threequarter Wall was constructed in the late nineteenth century. There is an animal pound on the north side and a stile near the west end.

'Mangonel' battery [108223]

The top of the cliff, just to the north of Halfway Wall, has been improved with a drystone wall to create a flat platform. Excavation in 1966 recovered thirteenth-century pottery leading to the suggestion that this was a platform to hold a mangonel, a large stone throwing machine, that was known to have been taken to Lundy in 1222. Whilst a nice story, the location seems rather precarious and would have been hard to manoeuvre a mangonel onto. It is perhaps more likely to have been a location for archers or musketeers to cover the approach from Jenny's Cove, probably from behind a wall or palisade that has now gone.

The wall supporting the platform known as the 'Mangonel' Battery, above Jenny's Cove

The footings of the wall surrounding the 'Mangonel' battery sometime after the excavation in 1966

Millstones [various]

At several places, the remains of millstone quarrying can be seen both on the top of the island, around Widows Tenement and on the west sidelands north of Jenny's Cove. There is a partly finished one by the west side track north of Threequarter Wall [108043], with adjacent circular hollows from which others have been taken. The date of these is not known, and as granite is not the best stone for milling, they may have been for apple crushers.

Millstone roughouts on the west sidelands north of Jenny's Cove

The most obvious of the millstones lies close to the west coast path, north of Threequarter Wall

'Blackhouse' [108150]

Keith Gardner excavated this site in 1967 which he compared to the blackhouses of the western and northern isles of Scotland. Records of his further excavation the following year do not appear to support this interpretation and it may be that there are two phases of building here that Gardner did not distinguish. No finds were recovered, suggesting that the site is medieval or earlier. Today it is hard to distinguish the archaeological remains from the grassed-over spoil heaps from the excavation.

The remains of the 'Blackhouse' excavated in 1967, from the north

Admiralty lookout [108183]

Often called Tibbetts after the hill on which it stands, this was built as an Admiralty lookout in 1909. It originally had a wooden second storey and a semaphore for signalling. The circular wall around it was built in 1990. Excavations for water supply and drainage have thrown up prehistoric pottery suggesting a burial mound or settlement stood here before the buildings.

The Admiralty Lookout after abandonment

Shipwrecks

Off Tibbetts Point are two protected wrecks. The Gull Rock wreck is believed to be that of a fifteenth- to sixteenth-century vessel and is represented only by cannon and stone cannon balls. The *Iona II* is much more recent, built in 1863 as a fast paddle-steamer for use on the Clyde. Her speed, partly based on a specially designed twin-cylinder oscillating engine, led to her purchase by an American, allegedly to act as a gun-runner for Confederate forces in the Civil War. She sank on her first voyage, heading for Madeira and across the Atlantic.

Another wreck lies 4.5km to the north east: the *South Australian*, which was built in 1868 and sank in 1889. She was of composite construction with timber planking on a wrought-iron frame which combined strength and low weight and gave these clipper ships great speed. She is the only early clipper to have been wrecked in English waters, though the *Cutty Sark*, built a year later, survives in dry-dock in London.

Cairn or windmill [108128]

South of Threequarter Wall is a prominent outcrop with an oval stony mound on top. This has a hollowed centre revealing several large granite slabs. It has been suggested that the stones represent the collapsed remains of a burial chamber or that they formed the foundations for a circular windmill tower. This is a very exposed site for a windmill, which would have to have been very sturdy to survive gales.

The cairn or windmill mound

Threequarter Wall [108122]

The newest of the walls dividing the island, built in the 1870s or 1880s as part of the agricultural improvements by a tenant farmer.

Widows Tenement [108075]

This is the best-preserved medieval site on Lundy. Just to the east of the track are the rectangular remains of a longhouse with opposed doors in the long sides. People would have lived in one (west) end, and animals over-wintered in the other. Clustered round the buildings are small fields, probably for stock-control or gardens. These all lie within a large enclosure that shows many variations suggesting that it may have originated in the prehistoric period and been reused. A small excavation at the south-west corner of the longhouse recovered both medieval and prehistoric pottery.

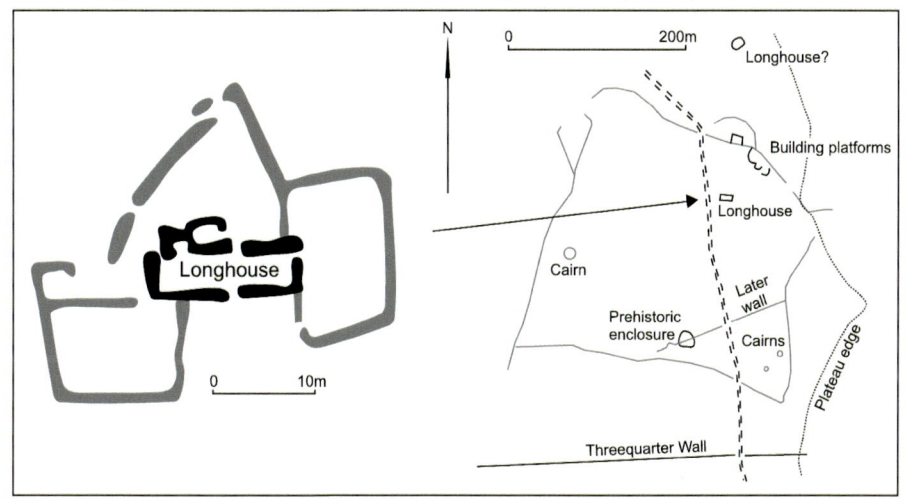

Plan of the Widows Tenement farmhouse (left) and large enclosure (right)

Brazen Ward [108048] *(plan opposite)*
Just above sea-level lie the ruins of a defensive structure blocking access from a slab of rock known as Frenchman's Landing. Much of the site appears to have collapsed into the sea but there is a wall, over 4m high on the seaward side, leading from the remains of what appears to be a tower or bastion. This has a narrow door, which has been walled-up. Further south are various other pieces of walling joining natural outcrops, and the 1886 Ordnance Survey map shows a small angle-bastion. The style of the defences suggests a sixteenth- or seventeenth-century date as does pottery recovered from a small excavation in the tower, although this does not date the original construction. It was not mentioned when Thomas Bushell was trying to reclaim expenses incurred during the Civil War, so may be Tudor in origin.

The wall running south from the tower at Brazen Ward

Bronze Age fields and houses [108019]
To the north of Gannets Combe is the best-preserved prehistoric settlement on the island with field walls surviving as low lines of stones. Attached to these are at least two round buildings, each with a rectangular annexe [108018, 108025]. Others were visible in the 1960s but have since become overgrown by heather. An excavation in one house recovered Middle Bronze Age pottery.

The ruins of a Bronze Age house [108018] on the east side. Two vertical stones define the doorway

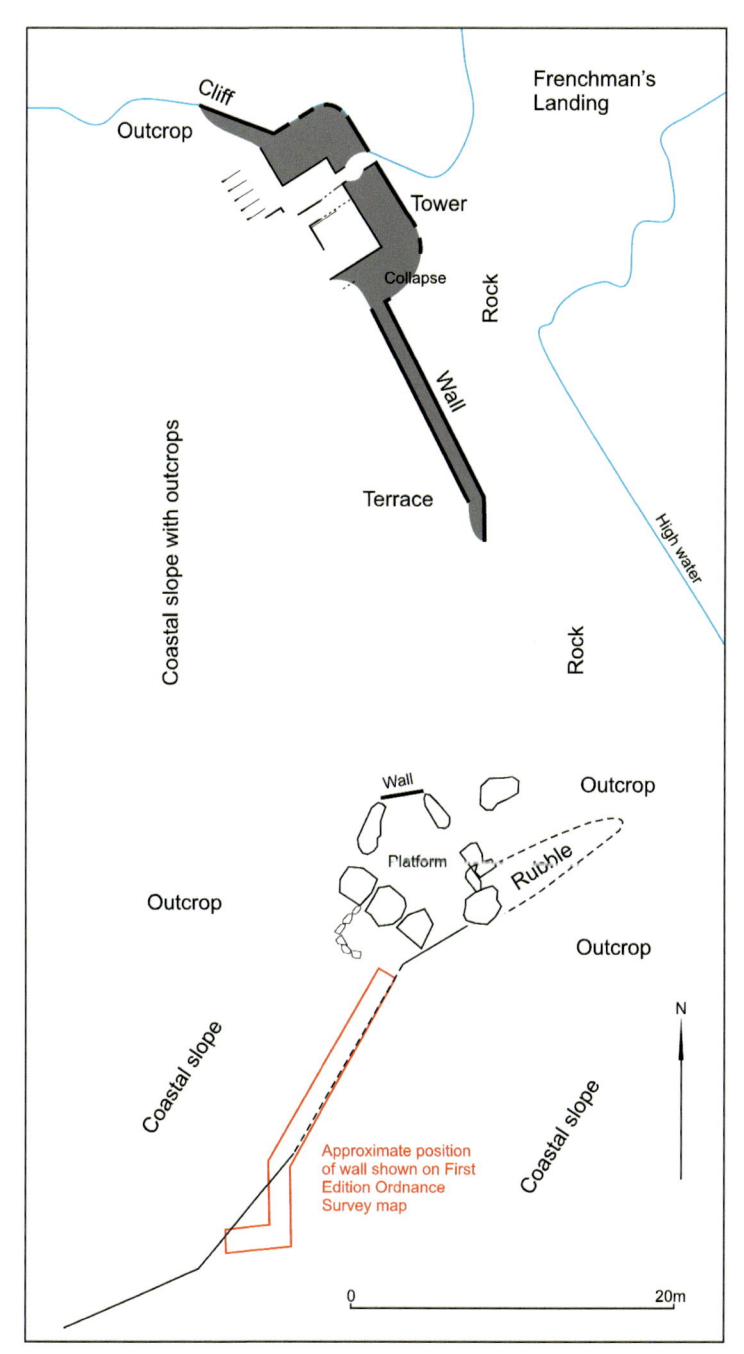

Plan of Brazen Ward

John O'Groats House [108008]

Above the North East Point are the ruins of a small building, possibly originally divided into two rooms, one with a fireplace. Its function is not certain; it may have been a base for shooting parties or possibly it was involved in the processing of seabirds for feathers and oil. The name is probably jocular, referring to its location in the far north.

John O'Groats House

Puffin Slope [108004]

Well down the slope is a small single-roomed building with a fireplace. It fills a level platform partly dug into the hillside and partly built out with a retaining wall. Its function is unclear but similar uses to John O'Groats House have been suggested. It is currently hard to access and this should not be attempted during the bird breeding season.

The Puffin Slope building with the fireplace to the right, the site of the doorway to the left and the retaining wall in the foreground

North East Battery [108006]

About 50m to the east of the Puffin Slope building is a level platform revetted by a drystone wall. It has been interpreted as a gun platform but seems rather too high above sea level for cannon to work effectively. It may have been associated with the seabird industry.

The North East Battery with rough retaining walls supporting a level platform

Acknowledgements

This booklet has been made possible by the help and encouragement of André Coutanche, Alan Rowland and Mandy Yates of the LFS and I thank them all. Design and layout was by André Coutanche. Any errors that remain are my own.

Chris Webster

Index of Sites

Acklands Moor .... page 18
Admiralty lookout .... page 24
Aircraft crash sites .... page 22
Anti-aircraft trenches .... page 14
Battery - see Fog Battery
Beacon Hill - see Cemetery on Beacon Hill
Benson's Cave .... page 11
'Blackhouse' .... page 24
Brazen Ward .... page 26
Bronze Age fields and houses .... page 26
Cairn or windmill .... page 25
Castle .... page 9
Cemetery on Beacon Hill .... page 15
Chambered tomb – the Kistvaen .... page 11
Fog Battery .... page 18
Giants Graves .... page 13
Golf Course - see Acklands Moor
Halfway Wall .... page 22
Heinkels - see Aircraft crash sites
HMS Montagu .... page 12
Hut circles - see Bronze Age fields and houses
John O'Groats House .... page 28
Kistvaen - see Chambered tomb – the Kistvaen
'Mangonel' battery .... page 22
Medieval farm .... page 21
Millstones .... page 23
Montagu - see HMS Montagu
New Town .... page 14
North East Battery .... page 29
Old Light .... page 14
Puffin Slope .... page 28
Punchbowl .... page 21
Quarries .... page 19
Quarter Wall .... page 19
Rocket Pole .... page 12
Shipwrecks .... page 24
Standing stones - see Acklands Moor
Threequarter Wall .... page 25
Tibbetts - see Admiralty Lookout
Village .... page 13
Widows Tenement .... page 25

Further information

THE Lundy Field Society maintains a comprehensive Lundy bibliography on its website *(www.lundy.org.uk)* where you can also access articles from the LFS's *Annual Report* (AR) and *Journal*. Other articles have been published in the *Devon Archaeological Society Proceedings* (DAS).

An overview of the prehistoric remains on Lundy can be found in Henrietta Quinnell's *Prehistoric and Roman material from Lundy*, DAS 68 (2010), 19-60. Short reports on the fieldwork that recovered many of those finds is reported by Keith Gardner in LFS AR 10, 11, 17 and 19. There are more detailed reports by John Schofield and Chris Webster on their 1980s fieldwork in LFS AR 39, 40 and 41 and Chris Webster has reviewed Gardner's original fieldwork records in LFS *Journal* 7.

Charles Thomas reported on the early Christian remains in LFS AR 20 and reinterpreted them in LFS AR 42. His book, *And Shall These Mute Stones Speak* (1994), has a chapter on the monastic activities on Lundy in relation to South Wales, Devon and Cornwall. Henrietta Quinnell reviewed Charles Thomas's work in 'Before the Early Christian cemetery site on Lundy', chapter 6 of Andy M Jones and Henrietta Quinnell, *An Intellectual Adventurer in Archaeology: Reflections on the Work of Charles Thomas* (2018).

There is a brief note on the medieval remains at Widows Tenement and the 'Mangonel battery' in LFS AR 17 with more details and interpretation in LFS *Journal* 7.

The medieval and later pottery from the village is reported by John Allan and Shirley Blaylock in *Medieval pottery and other finds from Pig's Paradise, Lundy*, DAS 63 (2005), 65-91. There is a report on the work at the Castle keep by Stephen Dunmore: *The castle in the isle of Lundy*, DAS 40 (1982), 153-62 but the National Trust's excavations remain unpublished. Benson's Cave is discussed by Tony Langham in LFS AR 40 and Myrtle Ternstrom provides an overview of the castle area in *The Castle on the Island of Lundy: 750 years, 1244-1994* (1994).

The LFS's work at Brazen Ward was reported in LFS AR 19 and reconsidered by Chris Webster in LFS *Journal* 7 which also covers the sites at Puffin Slope, John O'Groats House and the North East Battery.

The Old Light and later lighthouses are considered by Bob Farrah, a former lighthouse keeper, in LFS AR 44 and also by Myrtle Ternstrom in *Light over Lundy* (2007).

The Quarries are discussed by Langham in LFS AR 17 and more comprehensively by Peter Rothwell and Myrtle Ternstrom in *The Lundy Granite Company, an industrial adventure* (2008).

In 2006, Keith Gardner privately published *An Archaeologist on Lundy*, his frank, witty and irreverent memoirs.

There are displays and some archaeological artefacts in the museum in the village.

LUNDY FIELD SOCIETY
for the study and conservation of a unique island

Established 1946
Registered Charity 258294
www.lundy.org.uk

THE LUNDY FIELD SOCIETY (LFS) is a registered charity for the study of the archaeology, history and natural history of Lundy, and the conservation of its wildlife and antiquities.

Lundy is unique in many ways. It is home to an unusual range of plants, birds and other wildlife and, having suffered little disturbance, it offers special opportunities for study and research.

The island has a long and interesting history, with Bronze Age settlements, rare early Christian grave stones, a medieval castle and the remains of Victorian granite quarries. There is also a lot more architecture than you might expect!

There are 41 scheduled sites and monuments and 14 listed buildings. Much of the island is a Site of Special Scientific Interest (SSSI). The surrounding seas were the UK's first Marine Nature Reserve (now Marine Protected Area) and are a Special Area of Conservation.

The Lundy Field Society works with the island management. As well as providing volunteers for working holidays several times a year to assist the Lundy Conservation Team, we organise occasional events on the island which are open to our members, to islanders and to visitors.

The Lundy Field Society produces many publications, both regular ones for members, and books and leaflets for the general public. For more information about the Society, visit the the website at *www.lundy.org.uk*.

To join the LFS, fill in the online form or download a membership leaflet from *www.lundy.org.uk/lfs/join.html*. Whether you have just discovered Lundy or have known it for years, you will be welcomed as a member, and you will be making an important contribution to the study and conservation of the island through your membership.